Confident

'In a season that has been marked by darkness and suffering, it can be easy to ask "Where is God?" This beautiful collection of thirty devotionals tackles that question head on and draws deeply from the Scriptures to help to build our confidence in God. We may not know what the future holds, but *Confident* helps to remind us why we can utterly trust in the character of the God who walks with us into it.'
Andy Bannister, Director, Solas Centre for Public Christianity

'Stop digging around in the dirt! Here are wonderful truths to trust in, from key and much loved Bible passages. Your eyes and heart will be lifted to the great God of heaven and earth, to the saving work of Christ, and to his forgiveness, love, authority and sovereignty. Daily, you will be enabled to stand firm, whatever difficulties you face, confident of God's purposes for you as he gives you his grace and assurance of a glorious future ahead. Look to God's Word, look up and look forward; it is timeless but timely, and so helpful.'
Elinor Magowan, FIEC Women's Ministry Coordinator

30-DAY DEVOTIONAL

Confident

Edited by Elizabeth McQuoid

FOOD
FOR THE
JOURNEY

INTER-VARSITY PRESS
36 Causton Street, London SW1P 4ST, England
Email: ivp@ivpbooks.com
Website: www.ivpbooks.com

First published 2021

British Library Cataloguing-in-Publication Data
A catalogue record for this book is available from the British Library.

ISBN: 978–1–78974–190–2
eBook ISBN: 978–1–78974–189–6

Set in Avenir 11/15pt
Typeset in Great Britain by CRB Associates, Potterhanworth, Lincolnshire
Printed in Great Britain by Ashford Colour Press Ltd, Gosport, Hampshire

Inter-Varsity Press publishes Christian books that are true to the Bible and that communicate the gospel, develop discipleship and strengthen the church for its mission in the world.

IVP originated within the Inter-Varsity Fellowship, now the Universities and Colleges Christian Fellowship, a student movement connecting Christian Unions in universities and colleges throughout Great Britain, and a member movement of the International Fellowship of Evangelical Students. Website: www.uccf.org.uk. That historic association is maintained, and all senior IVP staff and committee members subscribe to the UCCF Basis of Faith.

Contributors

Psalm 23
Keith Weston
Keith was Rector of St Ebbe's Church, Oxford (1964–1985). He was also chair of the Keswick Convention Council and a trustee of UCCF (Universities and Colleges Christian Fellowship). He spoke at conventions associated with Keswick Convention around the world and at many university missions.

Psalms 93 and 94, Philippians 2, Colossians 3 and 1 Thessalonians 2
Alec Motyer
Alec was Vice Principal of Clifton Theological College, Bristol, and Vicar of St Luke's Church, Hampstead, before becoming Principal of Trinity College, Bristol. He was much loved on both sides of the Atlantic as a Bible expositor and a prolific author.

Psalm 121
Andrew Dow
Andrew trained for ministry at Oak Hill College, London. He and his wife Miriam served together in six UK churches

before moving to Stratford-upon-Avon, where Andrew is honorary Assistant Minister at Holy Trinity Church.

Habakkuk 2 and Revelation 2 and 4
Jonathan Lamb

Jonathan is Minister-at-Large for Keswick Ministries. He was previously CEO of Keswick Ministries and Director of Langham Preaching. He is the author of a number of books, including *Preaching Matters: Encountering the living God* and *Essentially One: Striving for the unity God loves*. He is also Vice President of IFES (International Fellowship of Evangelical Students).

Romans 8:28–30
Vaughan Roberts

Vaughan has been Rector of St Ebbe's Church, Oxford, since 1998. He is Director of Proclamation Trust, an organization that encourages and equips Bible teachers, and the author of many books, including *God's Big Picture: A Bible overview* and *Battles Christians Face*.

Romans 8:31–39
Alistair Begg

Alistair is from Scotland, but has been Senior Pastor at Parkside Church, Cleveland, Ohio, USA, since 1983. He is the voice behind the daily radio broadcast *Truth for Life* and has written a number of books, including *Pray Big: Learn to pray like an apostle.*

Colossians 1
Steve Brady
Steve has spoken at conferences and conventions around the world, many linked to the Keswick Convention, of which he was a trustee and speaker for two decades. He held four pastorates in the UK before becoming Principal of Moorlands College, Sopley, Dorset. He is now Senior Pastor at First Baptist Church, Grand Cayman, West Indies.

1 John 4
Hugh Palmer
Hugh was Vicar of Christ Church, Fulwood, Sheffield, from 1997 to 2005. He then served as Rector of All Souls Church, Langham Place, London, and was a chaplain to the Queen. He is Chair of Word Alive.

Revelation 1
Raymond Brown
Formerly Principal of Spurgeon's College, London, Raymond also served as a Baptist minister in Cambridge and Torquay. He is the author of a number of books, including several volumes in IVP's The Bible Speaks Today series.

Preface

What is the collective name for a group of preachers? A troop, a gaggle, a chatter, a pod . . . ? I'm not sure! But in this Food for the Journey series we have gathered an excellent group of Bible teachers to help us to unpack the Scriptures and understand some of the core issues that every Christian needs to know.

Each book is based on a particular theme and contains excerpts from messages given by much loved Keswick Convention speakers, past and present. When necessary, the language has been updated but, on the whole, this is what you would have heard had you been listening in the tent on Skiddaw Street. A wide, though not exhaustive, selection of Bible passages explores the key theme, and each day of the devotional ends with a fresh section on how to apply God's Word to your own life and situation.

Whether you are a Convention regular or have never been to Keswick, this Food for the Journey series provides a unique opportunity to study the Scriptures and a particular topic with a range of gifted Bible teachers by your side. Each book is designed to fit in your jacket pocket or handbag, so that you can read it anywhere – over the breakfast table, on the commute into work or college, while you are waiting in your car, during your lunch break or in bed at night. Wherever life's journey takes you, time in God's Word is vital nourishment for your spiritual journey.

Our prayer is that these devotionals become your daily feast, a nourishing opportunity to meet with God through his Word. Read, meditate on, apply and pray through the Scriptures given for each day, and allow God's truths to take root and transform your life.

If these devotionals whet your appetite for more, there is a 'For further study' section at the end of each book. You can also visit our website <www.keswickministries.org/resources> to find the full range of books, study guides, CDs, DVDs and mp3s available.

Let the word of Christ dwell in you richly.
(Colossians 3:16, ESV)

Introduction
Unshakeable confidence

'We died before we came here,' Stephen Foreman often reminded his wife Emily, as they adjusted to the major challenges of missionary life in the inhospitable deserts of North Africa.

The Foreman family had traded comfort, security and the American dream to share the gospel in a 100% Islamic country. Stephen and Emily had calculated that any sacrifice was worth making to glorify God and reach the Muslim people with the gospel. On 25 June 2010, at the age of 39, Stephen paid the ultimate price when he was shot and killed by al-Qaeda operatives (Emily Foreman, *We Died Before We Came Here*, NavPress, 2016).

Stephen lived – and died – by this conviction: 'I have been crucified with Christ and I no longer live, but Christ lives in me' (Galatians 2:20).

But how could he be so confident, so sure of God's purposes and promises? So sure, in fact, that he would risk life itself? Why would so many others do the same thing?

Biblical confidence does not mean that we don't shed tears, ask questions or have doubts. It certainly doesn't mean that God helps us to grow in our popularity or assertiveness. Biblical confidence means that we trust God's character and his Word completely.

This confidence in who God is and what he has said means that, even in the darkest days – when we face suffering, when our prayers seem unanswered, when it doesn't look as if God is in control – we can trust him.

So . . .

- when we are riddled with doubts, we can be confident in our salvation;

- when we face suffering, we can be confident that God still loves us;

- when we share our faith, we can be confident in the truth and reliability of God's Word;

- when we are dealing with disappointment, we can be confident that God is for us and working on our behalf;

- when we are worried about the future, we can be confident of our eternal destiny;

- when our circumstances are spiralling out of control, we can be confident that God is sovereign;

- when we sin or give in to temptation, we can be confident that if we turn to God in repentance, he will forgive us.

Of course, when these things happen, and when God withdraws 'the light of his countenance'[1] from us and circumstances stack up against us, we often struggle to trust him. Confidence in God's character and his Word seem to slip away like sand through our fingers. The devil enjoys nothing more than stealing our assurance from us, like a magician pulling a tablecloth from under cups and saucers.

Is there anything we can do to recover our confidence? Biblical confidence is a gift from God. He gives the Holy Spirit to testify to our spirits that we belong to him and are loved by him. He whispers the truth to our souls. But being confident is not a passive thing, not merely a gift to receive. We cultivate assurance, which grows stronger as we love and follow Christ. The more we pray, meet God in the Scriptures, obey him and prove his faithfulness, the greater our confidence in him becomes.

The apostle John reminds us, 'We know that we have come to know him if we keep his commands' (1 John 2:3; see also 2 Peter 1:4–11). Obedience to God's Word becomes a means to obtain confidence in our faith, as well as evidence of it. Our gradual transformation to become more like Christ is proof that the gospel is true and God is at work. Even hardships don't have to rock our confidence; they can give it deeper roots, if we view them as opportunities to see God's faithfulness and take him at his word.

This devotional draws on a wide variety – though not an exhaustive list – of Bible passages to renew our confidence in the unshakeable truths of God's Word and the unchanging nature of his character. It is an invitation to 'stand firm and hold fast' (2 Thessalonians 2:15) to God himself. Each day provides an opportunity to enjoy a deeper, richer experience of the 'full assurance that faith brings' (Hebrews 10:22).

Note

1. From the *Westminster Confession* (1646), XVIII: iv.

Psalms

Imagine being able to sing the songs Jesus sang or pray the prayers he prayed. Well, you can! Jesus, like many Israelites before and after him, used the psalms in public and private worship. The Old Testament book of Psalms is a collection of prayers and songs, gathered over a number of centuries and written by a variety of authors, including King David. Each one is carefully crafted poetry, rich in imagery and, although written for a specific context, contains timeless truths. On any and every occasion, we can go to the psalms to find words to express our emotions, words of Scripture we can use to speak to God.

The psalms teach us that God is our King, Creator, Judge, Redeemer, Helper and Deliverer. We can be completely confident in his love, care, commitment and protection. In life and in death, God is with us and sufficient to meet all our needs.

Day 1

Read Psalm 23
Key verses: Psalm 23:1–3

....

¹The LORD is my shepherd, I lack nothing.
  ²He makes me lie down in green pastures,
he leads me beside quiet waters,
  ³he refreshes my soul.
He guides me along the right paths
  for his name's sake.

Are you confident that you have everything you need?

Satan has an arsenal of weapons at his disposal. One of his most popular tactics is to peddle the lie that if we yield ourselves to Christ completely, we will suffer incalculable loss. But we will not! Far from wanting to strip us of everything worthwhile in this life, the Good Shepherd wants to clothe us in riches. Indeed, when Jesus is our Shepherd, when we surrender ourselves to his lordship, we can say for certain, 'I shall not want' (Psalm 23:1, ESV).

How is it that we will lack nothing? Because the Shepherd is lord of infinite grace. In Psalm 34:10, David says, 'Those who seek the LORD lack no good thing.' In Romans 8:32, the apostle Paul adds, 'He who did not spare his own Son, but gave him up for us all – how will he not also, along with him, graciously give us all things?' In the magnificent opening of the letter to the Ephesians, Paul presses home the point: 'Praise be to the God and Father of our Lord Jesus Christ, who has blessed us in the heavenly realms with every spiritual blessing in Christ' (Ephesians 1:3). What an astonishing statement. He *has* blessed us – already – with every spiritual blessing that he has to give us. When we become Christians, we are united to Christ and that union means we receive every spiritual blessing available in the heavenly realms.

Peter writes, 'His divine power has given us everything we need for a godly life through our knowledge of him who called us by his own glory and goodness' (2 Peter 1:3). He makes over his riches to me now – in my situation – by refreshing my soul, by leading me by quiet waters and along the right paths (Psalm 23:2–3). He does this day by day, for his own name's sake, which means for his own honour and glory. If the Lord is your Shepherd, he has blessed you with every blessing; he calls you to surrender yourself to him and to enter into the fullness of those blessings. We can go all through life, to the grave and into eternity, and we will never exhaust the riches that are ours in Christ.

You may think that you lack many things – a spouse, children, health, finances, qualifications, recognition . . . To be without these things may be a source of pain, sadness and stress. But the Chief Shepherd invites you to follow him and find in him all the sustenance you need. Whatever your circumstances, you are rich beyond compare because you have every spiritual blessing in Christ. Today, keep your eyes on your Shepherd and allow him to refresh your soul. Listen to his voice through his Word and receive his limitless grace.

Day 2

Read Psalm 23
Key verse: Psalm 23:4

....

Even though I walk
    through the darkest valley,
I will fear no evil,
    for you are with me;
your rod and your staff,
    they comfort me.

Are you, or is someone you love, walking through the 'darkest valley'?

Instead of 'darkest valley', some translations say 'valley of the shadow of death'. There are many dark valleys but, certainly, the valley of the shadow of death is the one we will all face if the Lord does not come back before we cross it. But the psalmist knows, even in death, that there is no need to fear because God is with him. Notice the change in pronoun from 'he leads me . . . he refreshes . . .

he guides me . . .' to 'you are with me' when the valley is reached – the relationship is even closer.

There is a related passage in Psalm 84:5–7:

Blessed are those whose strength is in you,
    whose hearts are set on pilgrimage.
As they pass through the Valley of Baka,
    they make it a place of springs;
    the autumn rains also cover it with pools.
They go from strength to strength,
    till each appears before God in Zion.

On their pilgrimage to Jerusalem, the Israelites passed through the Valley of Baka, a very dry and arid place, a 'dark valley', as Psalm 23 would say. What did they do? Did they just mope away their days in Baka? Did they turn bitter against the Lord and say, 'Why did you bring us here?' No, they made it a place of springs. They didn't sit idly under suffering but, we might say, they got out their shovels, dug wells and they found the grace of God. They went 'from strength to strength', and if the Lord had not led them through this valley, they would not have had their faith strengthened.

The end of verse 7 of Psalm 84 is reassuring. When you are going through the dark valley, God does not let go of you. He is with you 'till each appears before God in Zion'.

His rod and his staff are your comfort. He will be with you in the valley and see you through the other side, tried but purified. You do not need to worry because God knows the path you take, the God of all wisdom directs your life and he is with you.

'You are with me.' Let the implications of that phrase sink deep into your soul today. God is not with you as an observer. He is there to lead (Psalm 23:2), refresh (verse 3), guide (verse 3) and comfort you (verse 4). In the person of the Holy Spirit, the almighty God of the ages, your heavenly Father, is forever present with you.

You may be serving God in a difficult situation, laid low with depression or approaching that final valley of the shadow of death. Whatever your valley, do not fear; the Chief Shepherd is carrying you on his shoulders and he will not let you go (Luke 15:5).

Day 3

Read Psalm 23
Key verses: Psalm 23:5–6

•••

> ⁵*You prepare a table before me*
> *   in the presence of my enemies.*
> *You anoint my head with oil;*
> *   my cup overflows.*
> ⁶*Surely your goodness and love will follow me*
> *   all the days of my life,*
> *and I will dwell in the house of the LORD*
> *   for ever.*

Does your wandering heart sap your confidence in your salvation and your suitability for Christian service? How can you get back on track?

The key is the opening statement of Psalm 23: 'The LORD is my shepherd.' In Old Testament times, 'shepherd' was the word used for kings and leaders (see Ezekiel 34). So David, the writer of the psalm, is saying, 'The Lord is my king', and he is surrendering to the kingship – the rule, priorities and values – of the loving Shepherd. Those, like David, whose lives are shaped by the Shepherd acknowledge that God's goodness and mercy follow them all their days. The Hebrew verb for 'dwell' in verse 6 could be future as well as present tense. I imagine here a man or a woman who, all through the ups and downs of an earthly pilgrimage, dwells consciously in the presence of the Lord.

When I acknowledge that the Lord is my Shepherd, and that goodness and mercy are following me all the days of my life, it is more difficult to wander. I *want* to dwell in God's presence every day. I once was God's enemy but now he is the dearest friend that I have. The apostle Paul sums up our relationship with God in Romans 5:1–2: Jesus' death on the cross blots out past sin, and brings us peace and reconciliation with God. We have access to God's grace, which sustains in all the circumstances of life. And what's more, looking ahead to the future, I rejoice in my hope of sharing the glory of God, guaranteed for me by the Shepherd, whose goodness and mercy follow me all the days of my life until, at long last, I am home.

God knows that your heart wanders. But he welcomes you into his presence regardless. Today, reflect on all his goodness and mercy to you. Ask for renewed dedication to live under his lordship:

O to grace how great a debtor
Daily I'm constrained to be!
Let Thy goodness, like a fetter,
Bind my wandering heart to Thee.
Prone to wander, Lord, I feel it,
Prone to leave the God I love;
Here's my heart, O take and seal it,
Seal it for Thy courts above.
(Robert Robinson, 'Come, Thou fount of every blessing',
1758)

Thank God that, although we fail, the Chief Shepherd remains utterly committed to us:

My sheep listen to my voice; I know them, and they follow me. I give them eternal life, and they shall never perish; no one will snatch them out of my hand. My Father, who has given them to me, is greater than all; no one can snatch them out of my Father's hand.
(John 10:27–29)

Day 4

Read Psalm 93
Key verse: Psalm 93:1

. . . .

*The L*ORD *reigns, he is robed in majesty;*
*the L*ORD *is robed in majesty and armed with*
strength;
indeed, the world is established, firm and secure.

What picture do you have in mind when you imagine God?

Do you see a baby in a manger, a rugged Galilean or a bloody body on a cross? The psalmist wants us to visualize and remember that the Lord is King.

• *He is an eternal King*. Verses 1, 3 and 4 affirm the present reality of his kingship. In verse 2, we stand by the throne and realize that there has never been a time when the Lord wasn't King. And verse 5 points forward to the Lord being King for 'endless days'.

- *He is a reigning King.* In the opening verses of the psalm, we see the throne, and then we let our eyes drop beneath it to the world over which the King reigns. The clear implication is that the created order depends for its stability on the security and changelessness of a reigning King. Verse 3 depicts a turbulent world but, when we look beyond the reality of the pounding waves, we see what the Bible insists is equally a reality – a reigning God.

- *He is an active King.* The Lord's kingship is neither idle nor ornamental, but real and active. He is wearing the kingly robes of majesty (verse 1) to indicate his capacity and commitment to rule.

- *He is an absolute King.* The psalm doesn't mention where God reigns. He reigns over this world and holds it in his hand. Neither does the psalmist specify enemies. He portrays them with the single image of the turbulent sea. The message is that over all his enemies, regardless of who they are, the Lord on high is mighty.

In verses 2 and 5, the people acknowledge the Lord as their King. In response, in verse 5, they commit themselves to the truth and reliability of the word that God has spoken and which he has vouched for. They also commit themselves to the holiness that he requires. We can respond in the same way because we know that the Lord is King. This great truth is our shield and strength, the armour to face the daily challenges of life.

Are you caught up in those swirling waves of Psalm 93? Our struggles are real, but there is an unseen reality of which we can be sure: the Lord is King. Don't become discouraged. God knows what is going on in your life, he cares and he is in absolute control. Let this truth be your shield today.

> Blessed are you, Israel!
>> Who is like you,
>> a people saved by the LORD?
> He is your shield and helper
>> and your glorious sword.
> Your enemies will cower before you,
>> and you will tread on their heights.
> (Deuteronomy 33:29)

> We wait in hope for the LORD;
>> he is our help and our shield.
> (Psalm 33:20)

> You are my refuge and my shield;
>> I have put my hope in your word.
> (Psalm 119:114)

Day 5

Read Psalm 94
Key verse: Psalm 94:22

....

But the LORD has become my fortress,
and my God the rock in whom I take refuge.

'Your God doesn't care about what is going on in the world.'

How do you feel when people lambast God like this? In Psalm 94, God's people are dealing with enemies who were not afraid to speak against them, act with violence and hatred towards the helpless, and deny God's love. When we face similar opposition, this psalm bolsters our confidence by reminding us who God is.

• *We have a God of redemption.* In verse 5, the psalmist calls the Israelites 'your people'. They became God's people at the exodus, when he brought them out of Egypt. This was their redemption, when they were rescued from slavery. We too are the redeemed. We have been brought out of slavery to sin by Christ's blood, which was shed on the cross. And God cannot forget those for whom his Son died. His love will never fail us.

- *We have a God of creation.* God made the ear and eye (verse 9). The Bible tells us that the Creator is involved in his creation: he began all things, maintains all things, governs all things and guides all things to their appointed destiny. Can this God be absent or uninvolved?

- *We have a God of providence.* Verses 12–15 remind us of God's involvement, direction and control, even in the smallest details of the experiences of his people. In the thick of this hostility, the psalmist says, 'Blessed is the one you discipline' (verse 12). He speaks of this experience as purposeful: it is the way to peace, the loving way that God brings his people home, and a pit is being dug for the wicked (verse 13). Verse 14 emphasizes that, even in our present difficulties, we have an underlying confidence – 'the Lord will not reject his people'.

- *We have a God of tender care.* The psalmist found himself lonely (verses 16–17), dealing with the precariousness of life (verse 18) and afflicted with distracting thoughts, not knowing what to believe (verse 19). In those times, he found the Lord to be his help, support and comfort (verses 17–19). The New King James Version of the Bible says, 'Your comforts delight my soul.' This speaks of the indescribable inner communications of God whereby he comforts us.

• *We have a God of security and triumph*. God triumphs over the ungodly; he cuts them off. But, for the believer, there is complete security (verse 22). God is 'my fortress'. The Lord lifts his child up into a fortress because it is high and inaccessible to the enemy. He is also 'my . . . refuge' – he is there, available for me to run to.

Meditate on the character of God in Psalm 94. Whether you are suffering for being a Christian or simply because we live in a fallen world, rest secure in God's unfailing love, care, commitment and protection. Run to him; he is your refuge. Let him lift you up; he is your fortress. Surely, we say with the psalmist:

Who is like you, LORD God Almighty?
You, LORD, are mighty, and your faithfulness
surrounds you.
(Psalm 89:8)

Day 6

Read Psalm 121
Key verses: Psalm 121:7–8

••

⁷The LORD will keep you from all harm –
   he will watch over your life;
⁸the LORD will watch over your coming
      and going
   both now and for evermore.

Do you have confidence in God's promises?

Psalm 121 is full of big promises. In verses 3–6, we follow the pilgrims on their way to Jerusalem and in their nightly camping. When they are on the move, the psalmist affirms, '[God] will not let your foot slip', and when they are at rest, 'he who watches over you will not slumber'. In those days in Israel, you hired a keeper to watch over you while you slept. The trouble was that those hired keepers would sometimes fall asleep themselves. Not so the Lord! He is totally reliable.

God will protect us (verse 6). In Old Testament times, people believed that the moon shed malignant influences on unsuspecting sleepers. So, God promises protection from real perils, such as sunstroke, and imagined perils, such as those from the moon. He protects us from our fears, whether they are reasonable or groundless. God's cover is fully comprehensive.

Then the psalmist's enthusiasm seems to have run away with him: 'The LORD will keep you from all harm' (verse 7). But surely this promise doesn't hold true when we place it next to the realities of life? The Christian has no divine immunity from hurt or trouble. You've only got to read about the sufferings of the apostle Paul to understand that. So what does this promise mean? Paul's answer would be that the Christian can be sure that any so-called evil is good 'with a veil on'. That's his point in Romans 8:28: 'And we know that in all things God works for the good of those who love him, who have been called according to his purpose.' Even when the Christian cannot understand what God is doing, he or she knows that God's love is in, and behind, his work.

To paraphrase Psalm 121:7 slightly, 'The Lord will keep you from the ultimate corruption of evil', from the devil, if you like. Whatever is thrown at you, you will not sink without a trace because you are being kept by the Master

Keeper. This interpretation is supported by the second half of verse 7: 'he will watch over your life' – your soul, the deepest part of you. Jesus himself said not to worry about those who have the power to destroy the body; rather, fear the soul-keeper (Matthew 10:28). If you belong to God, he will keep your soul safe in this life and the next. That's a great assurance.

Insert your name into Psalm 121 and meditate on God's precious promises. He is watching over you and protecting you in ways that you may never know. In the face of overwhelming circumstances, know for sure that the devil's reach is limited. Cling to the certain hope that your soul is being kept by the Master Keeper.

Habakkuk

We don't often get an insight into a prophet's private prayer life. But in the book of Habakkuk, we see this prophet crying out to God. Habakkuk was a contemporary of Jeremiah and lived in Jerusalem. Under King Jehoiakim, wickedness, violence and anarchy were rife, and the prophet couldn't understand why God did not intervene. When God answered Habakkuk's prayer and told him judgment would come through the hands of the evil Babylonians, he was even more stunned.

What changed the questions 'Why?' and 'How long, Lord?' in chapter 1 to the worship of chapter 3? When God doesn't answer our prayers as we hoped he would, when we don't understand what he is doing, how can we, like Habakkuk, say with confidence, 'Yet I will rejoice in the LORD, I will be joyful in God my Saviour' (3:18)? This book teaches us how to be confident in God's character and purposes, regardless of our circumstances.

Day 7

Read Habakkuk 2:1–20
Key verses: Habakkuk 2:14, 20

. . . .

¹⁴For the earth will be filled with the knowledge
*of the glory of the L*ORD
as the waters cover the sea . . .

²⁰*The L*ORD *is in his holy temple;*
let all the earth be silent before him.

When your world is rocked by grief and loss, in whom or what do you put your confidence?

The prophet Habakkuk famously declared, 'Though the fig-tree does not bud and there are no grapes on the vines . . . yet I will rejoice in the LORD, I will be joyful in God my Saviour' (3:17, 18). But this declaration wasn't easy triumphalism. Habakkuk had wrestled with God to get to this point.

The first two chapters of the book see the prophet distraught at the violence and injustice in Judah, and wondering why God does not intervene. When God says he will send the Babylonians to judge the Israelites, Habakkuk is even more perplexed. How could a holy God appoint such an evil nation to execute judgment? They were even less righteous than the Israelites! In the midst of his despair, there are two shafts of light for Habakkuk (and for us) to cling to:

- *A present reality: 'The Lord is in his holy temple' (verse 20).* The Babylonians may be arrogantly asserting their power, but the Lord of the universe is reigning in the place of ultimate authority, high above his creatures. The deities that the pagans turn to are useless (verse 19), but God is in control and can be relied upon.

- *A future certainty: 'the earth will be filled with the knowledge of the glory of the Lord' (verse 14).* In the context of the power of empires and the pretension of human rulers, the Lord speaks of the certainty of what will be left on that final day: the universal knowledge of God. There is a similar phrase in Isaiah 11:9, when the prophet looked at that great messianic era, which pointed to Jesus himself, the One who would ultimately bring the victory of God's purposes, the destruction of evil, the salvation of his people, and the establishment of a new heaven and a new earth. Habakkuk adds the word 'glory' to Isaiah's phrase, perhaps because it encompasses the greatest goal of all human history – the glory of God. One day, all other glories will fade in the light of this supreme glory: his royal majesty. We can look forward to the final triumph of God, when the world will be filled with his purposes, presence and glory.

In the midst of suffering and grief, when all other certainties have been swept away, you can be confident that God is in control now and will ultimately triumph. These twin truths are like stakes in the ground, anchors that hold us fast in turbulent times. The psalmist captures the same truths for us to meditate on:

'Be still, and know that I am God;

I will be exalted among the nations,

I will be exalted in the earth.'

The Lord Almighty is with us;

the God of Jacob is our fortress.

(Psalm 46:10–11)

Romans

Paul had always longed to visit Rome. Probably during his third missionary journey, on the way back to Jerusalem, with the collection he'd received for the poverty-stricken believers, Paul wrote to the church in Rome, anticipating his visit. Because this church had never had a visit from an apostle, Paul was at pains to convey the basic truths of the gospel. He presented God's plan of salvation almost like a theological essay to this mixed congregation of Jews and Gentiles. Paul explained why Christians can be confident of God's love, certain that he will conform them to the likeness of Christ, secure in their salvation and the hope of final glory.

Day 8

Read Romans 8:18–30
Key verse: Romans 8:28

· ·

And we know that in all things God works for the good of those who love him, who have been called according to his purpose.

Have you ever heard this verse quoted glibly?

You have just received news that you've got an incurable disease or someone you love has died: 'Oh, don't worry . . .' and someone quotes verse 28. 'Praise the Lord, anyway.'

Taking this verse out of context makes light of very real suffering. Not all things are good for Christians, and some things we experience are very bad indeed: bereavement, sickness, the largely hidden pain of childlessness, unwanted singleness, a difficult marriage, the psychological scars of bullying, emotional or sexual abuse, the desperation of depression, or an estrangement from family or friends. It is not that all things are good but that, in all things, God works *for good*, fulfilling his purposes.

The big question is, of course, what is this good? Verse 27 says, 'The Spirit intercedes for God's people in accordance with the will of God.' The good is God's will, which is described in verses 29–30: 'For those God foreknew he also predestined to be conformed to the image of his Son' (verse 29). This is his will for our lives – that we might be like Jesus once again, perfectly conformed to his image, perfectly reflecting his glory. Verse 30 continues, 'Those he predestined, he also called; those he called, he also justified; those he justified, he also glorified.' These two verses span eternity. God has an eternal purpose for our lives and he will not let anything stop him fulfilling it. That doesn't remove the pain but it does give great perspective within it.

Terrible things may happen, but God is at work and forming us into the likeness of Jesus. Of course, there is mystery: 'Why did God allow that to happen to me?' Or sometimes, even harder to deal with, when it's someone we love very much: 'Why did God allow that to happen to him or her?' It doesn't make any sense, and sometimes we don't see any good come from it. But we can trust our Sovereign God, that in all things he is at work, conforming his people into the likeness of Christ.

You may be dealing with many things in your life that are not 'good'. Today, will you cling to the certainty that God is sovereign and working out his eternal purposes? Will you ask God to help you to accept your suffering as his instrument to make you more like Christ? More than that, with God's enabling, will you join him in his work and strive to grow in godliness, even in these dark days?

> Now may the God of peace, who through the blood of the eternal covenant brought back from the dead our Lord Jesus, that great Shepherd of the sheep, equip you with everything good for doing his will, and may he work in us what is pleasing to him, through Jesus Christ, to whom be glory for ever and ever. Amen.
> (Hebrews 13:20–21)

Day 9

Read Romans 8:18–30
Key verses: Romans 8:29–30

••

29For those God foreknew, he also predestined to be conformed to the image of his Son, that he might be the firstborn among many brothers and sisters. 30And those he predestined, he also called; those he called, he also justified; those he justified, he also glorified.

Are you confident that you will persevere in the Christian faith? Confident that you will be with Christ when you die?

Paul helps to answer these questions in verses 29–30, verses sometimes described as 'the golden chain'. It begins 'those whom God foreknew'. Paul is not speaking about the fact that God can tell in advance which choices we might make. This phrase speaks about an intimate, personal knowledge. God set his love on a group before they ever loved him, before they were ever born. The golden chain is not fastened ultimately by anything I do – if it were, it would be bound to break. It is fastened on God's gracious commitment. Before I was even born, God foreknew, and those whom he 'foreknew, he also predestined'. Having set his love on a people, he decided on his plan for them, and determined to fulfil it, that they might be conformed to the likeness of Jesus. 'Those he predestined, he also called' is not simply talking about putting out an invitation and nervously looking to see if anyone might respond. It speaks of listening to his voice – with God calling his own. 'Those he called, he also justified' – that we might be absolutely in the right with God. 'Those he justified, he also glorified' – it is as good as done; it is absolutely certain. He will keep us *all* the way.

There is great mystery in God's sovereignty. But it does not deny human responsibility; we must repent and believe. Neither does it excuse human passivity. We can't say, 'Oh, God will bring his own in; I don't have to pray or share the gospel.' God uses the prayers and proclamation of his people, and faithful preaching.

But I can be sure that if I have truly put my trust in Christ, I have been born again. The Spirit of God is in me and has given me a new heart, a new desire to please him, even though I don't do this as I should. I have a new intimacy, a sense that I'm a child of God. I can be sure that I am justified and will be glorified. Whatever happens in my life, I can be sure that all things work for good because all things lead to glory.

> Everything in these verses – all of God's work, his choosing you, predestining you, calling you, justifying you, sanctifying you, bringing you to final glory – is designed by God not mainly to make much of us, but to free us and fit us to enjoy making much of Christ forever. So I plead with you, set your mind's attention and your heart's affection on the glory of Christ, so that you will be changed from glory to glory into his image, so that you might fully enjoy what you were made for – making much of Christ.
>
> (Extract from a sermon by John Piper, 'Glorification: Conformed to Christ for the supremacy of Christ', 11 August 2002, <www.desiringgod.org>, accessed 23 November 2020)

Day 10

Read Romans 8:18–39
Key verses: Romans 8:31–32

....

[31]What, then, shall we say in response to these things? If God is for us, who can be against us? [32]He who did not spare his own Son, but gave him up for us all – how will he not also, along with him, graciously give us all things?

Are you confident that God is *for* you?

There is no uncertainty in this verse: the God who calls and justifies is on our side. Therefore, whatever opposition comes our way is ultimately of no account. Paul is not suggesting that the opposition does not exist. He does not ask the question 'Who can be against us?' because many people can be against us. The evil one is against us and our conscience often accuses us. Paul asks, '*If God is for us*, who can be against us?' (emphasis added). He is saying that if we take all that is against us and set it alongside the fact of God's abiding presence on our behalf, we gain a proper perspective.

This is a lesson that the armies of Israel needed to learn. It took David the shepherd boy to remind them that the giant Goliath was of no account. 'If God is for us, you are nothing, Goliath.' The cry of God's people all the way through the Old Testament was this: 'If the Lord had not been on our side, what would have happened to us?' (see Psalm 124:1–5).

Paul picks up that Old Testament principle and reality, and brings it home to the believers in his day. 'Let me prove that God is for you,' says Paul. Here is the evidence: 'He . . . did not spare his own Son' (Romans 8:32). When Jesus prayed in the Garden of Gethsemane, 'If you are willing, take this cup from me' (Luke 22:42), the Father did not remove the cup of bitterness from him, so that those who are in Jesus might be able to drink the cup of blessing. Isaiah 53 says it was the will of God to crush him. God did not spare him; instead, he gave him up for us as a substitute. But never think of Christ as an unwilling participant in the Father's plan.

> It is true that the Father gave the Son; it is equally true that the Son gave himself. We mustn't speak of God punishing Jesus, or of Jesus persuading God. We must never make

Christ the object of God's punishment, or God the object of Christ's persuasion. For the Father and Son are subjects, not objects, taking the initiative to save sinners.
(John Stott, *The Cross of Christ*, IVP, 2006)

If God be for us, then who *can* be against us?

When we face opposition for our faith, when our conscience accuses us, it is tempting to throw up our hands and wonder, 'Is God *really* for me?' The cross is God's definitive answer. Jesus' death, of course, was a once-in-a-lifetime event but God – Father, Son and Holy Spirit – is still 'for us', with the same degree of passion and commitment. So, fix your eyes on the cross – see there God's ultimate demonstration of what he thinks of you. Today, marvel with the psalmist: 'If the Lord had not been on our side, what would have happened to us?' (Psalm 124:1, adapted).

Day 11

Read Romans 8:18–39
Key verse: Romans 8:32

•••

He who did not spare his own Son, but gave him up for us all – how will he not also, along with him, graciously give us all things?

Do you remember when you were desperately hoping for a toy at Christmas and, as you removed the toy from the box, you saw the label 'Batteries not included'?

Your heart sank; you had this wonderful gift but it couldn't work. Without batteries, the gift was useless and you were left to your own devices.

That is certainly not a picture of what God has done for us in Jesus. Paul uses unassailable logic to make the point in verse 32 that if God has given us the greatest and the best gift in Jesus, he will not withhold all the gifts and blessings of grace that complete the work that his goodness has begun. In Christ, all the blessings are ours, and the story of our Christian experience includes all that accompanies the wonder of our salvation in the Lord Jesus Christ. Again, Paul is asking us to think – would God have given us his Son, sent him to the cross for us, and then be unwilling to give us all the things that accompany his purposes?

Incidentally, 'give us all things' (verse 32) is a dangerous phrase if it is unearthed from the context. 'All things' does not mean that because God gave us salvation in Christ, he will give us everything we want or everything we ask for. No. Paul's argument is that God will give us all the things that are necessary to accomplish his purpose of making us like Christ. He will give us all we need 'to be conformed to the image of his Son' (verse 29).

We, like those first-century believers, can be fully confident that God finishes what he starts: 'he who began a good work in you will carry it on to completion until the day of Christ Jesus' (Philippians 1:6).

We often abandon DIY or gardening projects halfway through. We get tired, overwhelmed or just plain bored. But God is not like us. Hebrews 12:2 calls him 'the pioneer and perfecter' (NIV) or 'the author and finisher' (NKJV) of our faith. He promises to finish the work he started in us. Reflect on all that God has done in your life so far – these are wonderful examples of God's faithfulness and guarantee that he will finish his work. He will never abandon you.

He will keep you strong to the end so that you will be free from all blame on the day when our Lord Jesus Christ returns. God will do this, for he is faithful to do what he says, and he has invited you into partnership with his Son, Jesus Christ our Lord.

(1 Corinthians 1:8–9, NLT)

May God himself, the God of peace, sanctify you through and through. May your whole spirit, soul and body be kept blameless at the coming of our Lord Jesus Christ. The one who calls you is faithful, and he will do it.

(1 Thessalonians 5:23–24)

Day 12

Read Romans 8:18–39
Key verses: Romans 8:33–34

....

33Who will bring any charge against those whom God has chosen? It is God who justifies. 34Who then is the one who condemns? No one. Christ Jesus who died – more than that, who was raised to life – is at the right hand of God and is also interceding for us.

Are you riddled with guilt, doubting that God can forgive your sin?

Satan comes in our imaginations and says to the Father, 'Look at that sinner. How can you declare this person justified?'

'Well, yes,' says the Father, 'this person is a sinner. The charges that you bring are valid. But will you look at my Son's hands and feet? Will you look at the wounds in his side? Who are you to condemn? It is Christ who justifies.'

Paul is not suggesting that no charge may be brought against us (verse 33). What he is saying is that any charge that is brought cannot stand because the case is closed. The verdict has been rendered. Indeed, Romans 8 begins: 'Therefore, there is now no condemnation for those who are in Christ Jesus.' Why? Because, having been justified by faith, we have peace with God. Remember the great exchange – all our demerits to Christ's account and all Christ's righteousness to our account? The righteousness that God requires of us, if we are ever to stand before him, is the righteousness that God reveals in the work of the gospel, the righteousness that Christ has achieved on our behalf and the righteousness that God bestows upon all who believe.

'Christ Jesus who died – more than that, who was raised to life.' Verse 34 is simply stating the facts: we serve a risen Saviour. What possible good would a dead one be? It is as the risen Christ, the living Lord, that Christ ensures the security of all who are in him. It is as if Paul is saying in these verses, 'The reason why I am able to say these things (about no condemnation, the reality of justification and the irrelevance of someone who comes to accuse you) is because we are dealing with Christ Jesus who died an atoning death, who was raised to life and is seated at the right hand of God.' Jesus is in the place of dominion and authority. He is physically present in heaven, interceding for us. Not only does the Holy Spirit intercede concerning the groanings in our hearts but Jesus also intercedes on our behalf on the basis of his once-for-all work of atonement. He continues to secure all the benefits of his death for his people.

Are you hanging on to guilt, raking over failures and believing Satan's accusations? Why are you remembering sins that God has chosen to forget? Today, take God at his word. Jesus' death and resurrection have dealt with your sins – past, present and future – once and for all. Will you trust that Jesus' blood was sufficient to wipe away your sin? Consider the psalmist's words:

He does not treat us as our sins deserve
    or repay us according to our iniquities.
For as high as the heavens are above the earth,
    so great is his love for those who fear him;
as far as the east is from the west,
    so far has he removed our transgressions from us.
(Psalm 103:10–12)

Day 13

Read Romans 8:18–39
Key verse: Romans 8:35

••

Who shall separate us from the love of Christ? Shall trouble or hardship or persecution or famine or nakedness or danger or sword?

Do you truly believe that God loves you?

When difficulties or suffering come, we often think, 'If God really loved me, he wouldn't allow this to happen.' But Paul turns our argument on its head and asks in verse 35, 'Who shall separate us from the love of Christ?' or 'What shall separate us from the love of Christ?' Then he lists enemies of our happiness and potential security in Christ. Once again, he returns to the sufferings that he mentioned at the very beginning, the sufferings of this present time. Trouble, hardship, persecution, famine, nakedness, danger and sword – Paul lists them all.

In verse 36, he quotes Psalm 44:22, underlining the fact that suffering has always been part of the experience of God's people. Without a theology of suffering, we will fall prey to all kinds of temptation, and we will find it far more difficult to speak to sufferers who come to our churches.

Remember the prophet Jeremiah's words:

I have been deprived of peace;
    I have forgotten what prosperity is.
So I say, 'My splendour is gone
    and all that I had hoped from the LORD.'

I remember my affliction and my wandering,
    the bitterness and the gall.
I well remember them,
    and my soul is downcast within me.
Yet this I call to mind
    and therefore I have hope:

Because of the LORD's great love we are not consumed,
    for his compassions never fail.
They are new every morning;
    great is your faithfulness.
I say to myself, 'The LORD is my portion;
    therefore I will wait for him.'
(Lamentations 3:17–24)

Paul reinforces Jeremiah's point: 'Life is hard but God is good.'

Suffering doesn't separate us from God's love; in a strange way, it is proof of it. God longs for us to be like Christ. Suffering, if we allow it, imprints the likeness of Christ on us more deeply, as it forces us to rest, hope and trust in God alone.

John Newton, the former slave trader and author of the hymn 'Amazing grace', helps us to understand this:

> Assurance grows by repeated conflict, by our repeated experimental proof of the Lord's power and good-ness to save; when we have been brought very low and helped, sorely wounded and healed, cast down and raised again, have given up all hope, and been suddenly snatched from danger, and placed in safety; and when these things have been repeated to us and in us a thousand times over, we begin to learn to trust simply to the word and power of God, beyond and against appearances: and this trust, when habitual and strong, bears the name of assurance; for even assurance has degrees.
>
> (Tony Reinke, *Newton on the Christian Life*, Crossway, 2015, p. 220)

Day 14

Read Romans 8:18–39
Key verses: Romans 8:35–37

....

³⁵*Who shall separate us from the love of Christ? Shall trouble or hardship or persecution or famine or nakedness or danger or sword?* ³⁶*As it is written:*

'For your sake we face death all day long;
   we are considered as sheep to be
      slaughtered.'

³⁷*No, in all these things we are more than conquerors through him who loved us.*

Do you feel like a conqueror? Always, sometimes, almost never? (Delete as appropriate.)

The apostle Paul was very familiar with suffering and, as he rehearses the catalogue of difficulties that Christian believers face, he makes this amazing declaration: 'We are more than conquerors' (verse 37). The Greek word is *hypernikomen*, which sounds like some sort of computer game. Paul loads this word up: 'We are not just conquerors; we are more than conquerors. We are hyper-conquerors!' Now the reason why he uses this word is that it is the only word which does justice to the victory that is ours in the face of overwhelming odds. I am a hyper-conqueror in all the suffering and hardships outlined in verse 35.

But how can I be a conqueror in them? *In* them, *through* him – prepositions are important. In all these things I am more than a conqueror *through* him; 'through him who loved us' – a love that has been demonstrated in the cross, a love that is sustaining and everlasting. It is not that he started to love us and then he stopped along the way or that his love is a diminishing love. His love knows no end. There is no possibility of his baling out on us.

Therefore, even though all hell can be set loose against us – the accusations of conscience, the challenges of life, the immensity of the diminution of physical powers, the loss of personal relationships, the disintegration that comes by way of the ravages of sin – 'In all these things I am more than a conqueror through him who continues to love us.'

Troubles will come, but you can be confident of this: you can face illness, slurs on your reputation, grief – in fact, all things – not by gritting your teeth and willing yourself to press on, or by relying on a fantastic network of family and friends, but through Christ. Encouragement and the love of friends are valuable but, ultimately, the only way we can stand in the face of suffering is through Christ who continues to love us. Whatever happens to us, Jesus' life, death and resurrection guarantee his forever love for us.

Today, you will be a conqueror – not by gliding through your 'to do' list, avoiding problems or bypassing sorrow, but through Christ, secure in his love. With Paul, we can say:

I have been crucified with Christ and I no longer live, but Christ lives in me. The life I now live in the body, I live by faith in the Son of God, who loved me and gave himself for me.
(Galatians 2:20)

Day 15

Read Romans 8:18–39
Key verses: Romans 8:38–39

....

38For I am convinced that neither death nor life, neither angels nor demons, neither the present nor the future, nor any powers, 39neither height nor depth, nor anything else in all creation, will be able to separate us from the love of God that is in Christ Jesus our Lord.

Imagine trying to fly a plane through turbulence only by looking out of the window. You would be terrified; you wouldn't even know whether or not you were flying upside down. It is vital that the pilot flies while looking at the instruments because they tell the truth. The same applies in life: we must live not according to our feelings but by what we know to be true.

In this great declaration, Paul speaks of what he knows: 'I am convinced'. In the King James Version of the Bible, it says, 'I am persuaded'; in the English Standard Version, it is 'I am sure'. And it is a great encouragement when those to whom we look feel very confident about things. The early believers in Rome, reading this letter, would have been encouraged because, for them, tribulation, peril, sword and famine were not issues that they read about in missionary biographies – they were present realities. It would have been a tremendous encouragement for them to say, 'The one who is writing this letter to us knows about suffering, and he is convinced by the facts. He is persuaded by the truthfulness of what he knows.'

Paul says, 'I am sure that nothing can, and nothing will, separate us from God's love.' Then he runs through a list of potential or actual adversaries. 'Death nor life' – life, with all its battles, potential triumphs or temptations, and death, like an ever-rolling stream. We are either dead or alive; there is no middle ground. But the good news is that neither death nor life is going to separate you from God's love. 'Angels nor demons' – through the cross, Jesus has disarmed the powers of the unseen heavenly realms, whether they are of spiritual benefit or spiritual wickedness. 'Neither the present nor the future' – in other words, time is not going to erode God's love. The issues of time and space will not be able to impinge upon this. No chance. God is sovereign over both. 'Nor any powers' – don't worry about the forces of the universe or anything else in all creation. Nothing can – nothing will – 'separate us from the love of God, which is in Christ Jesus our Lord' (verse 39).

Are you convinced of God's love for you? As Christians, we may verbally assent to this truth but we don't always live as if we believe it. Our choices, priorities and behaviour are easily swayed by our feelings, circumstances and the opinions of others. How different would your life look if it were based on the same certainty Paul's was? If you were convinced of God's love for you, in what ways would it have an impact on the following aspects of your life?

- How you feel about yourself, your suffering and your failures.
- Your devotional life and prayers.
- Your relationships with family, friends and non-Christians.
- Your involvement at work and in church.

Philippians, Colossians and 1 Thessalonians

Philippians

Paul is writing to the church in the Roman colony of Philippi to thank them for their financial gift and update them on his work. He writes about a wide range of issues related to Christian living. He exhorts them to 'rejoice in the Lord' (4:4), live in humility and unity, and stand firm in the face of persecution. He warns them against legalists and libertines, and prays that the love they have for one another will continue to grow.

Crucially, Paul reminds these first-century believers – and us – that they can be confident that God is faithful and always accomplishes his purposes. This means that he will complete the work he started in their lives and conform them to the likeness of Christ – complete sanctification is guaranteed.

Colossians

There was a plethora of gods and spiritual beings to worship in Colossae. New Christians were encouraged to supplement their faith by turning to other powers and authorities. Paul wrote from his prison cell in Rome to assure them that Jesus is enough – Christ is pre-eminent and totally sufficient for every need. Paul urged the Colossians not to be swayed by other world views, nor to try to appease other gods, by reminding them that their identity was secure in Christ: 'your life is now hidden with Christ in God' (3:3). Like the Colossians, because of our union with Christ, we can be confident that we belong to God and our salvation is secure – now and for eternity.

1 Thessalonians

This epistle is essentially a follow-up letter to new Christians. Persecution had forced Paul and his companions to flee the busy seaport city of Thessalonica sooner than he would have wished, leaving a group of very new Jewish and Gentile converts (Acts 17:1–10). Paul wrote to these believers, encouraging them to stand firm in the midst of persecution. He also provided instruction about the second coming of Christ, which he had hoped to give in person. He prayed that, as they had started off so well, they would continue to make spiritual progress. These Thessalonians – and every other believer – could be confident in God's sovereignty. Satan's power is limited and God is looking after his church.

Day 16

Read Philippians 2:1–13
Key verses: Philippians 2:12–13

....

12Therefore, my dear friends, as you have always obeyed – not only in my presence, but now much more in my absence – continue to work out your salvation with fear and trembling, 13for it is God who works in you to will and to act in order to fulfil his good purpose.

If you are a child of God, God dwells in you.

'Christ in you, the hope of glory' is a present reality, not wishful thinking (Colossians 1:27). It is not a promise dependent on something else happening, not a challenge requiring you to do anything, but a fact to believe.

God is not in us like a guest or a lodger but as a worker. The verb 'works' in Philippians 2:13 conveys the sense that he works ceaselessly. At any moment of day or night, throughout all your life as a Christian, God is at work.

Other Bible verses that mention God's indwelling presence urge us to respect and reverence his holiness, such as Ephesians 4:30: 'do not grieve the Holy Spirit'. Clearly, the Christian who persists in sin is countering the action of God. However, the point of Philippians 2:13 is that, although we sin, God will never give up on us. That does not excuse our sin; it means that he stays faithful.

God works 'to will and to act in order to fulfil his good purpose' (Philippians 2:13). There are two sides to every action. There is the decision and there is the bringing it to pass. There is the will and the action. We are often so weak that we cannot even choose what is right. Sometimes, we can choose what is right but we can't make it happen. But God does both. His work is effective. God will accomplish his purpose; his work will achieve what it was designed to do. Philippians 3:21 explains that God has 'power that enables him to bring everything under his control'. The God who is working in us is conforming all things to his will – and that includes you!

Are you worried that God has abandoned you, that your sin and failure have finally pushed him away? God has not given up on you. He has promised to keep working in you to make you increasingly like Jesus. The challenge is this: will you join him in his work?

God wants you to be holy. Through faith, He already counts you holy in Christ. Now He intends to make you holy with Christ. This is no optional plan . . . God saved you to sanctify you. God is in the beautification business, washing away spots and smoothing out wrinkles. He will have a blameless bride. He promised to work in you; He also calls you to work out. 'The beauty of holiness' is first of all the Lord's (Ps. 29:2, KJV). But by His grace it can also be yours.

(Kevin DeYoung, *The Hole in Our Holiness*, Crossway, 2012, p. 146)

Day 17

Read Philippians 2:1–13
Key verses: Philippians 2:12–13

....

12Therefore, my dear friends, as you have always obeyed – not only in my presence, but now much more in my absence – continue to work out your salvation with fear and trembling, 13for it is God who works in you to will and to act in order to fulfil his good purpose.

Are you confident by now that God is at work in you, and using all the circumstances of your life to make you more like Jesus?

Imagine if God waited for our permission before he acted. There might be a few days a month when we would be fired up for God to work, but the rest of the time we might not be so keen. Thankfully, God is not waiting for our assent. Paul makes it clear that God is working to 'fulfil his good purpose'. Another Bible version, the King James Version, says he is working for 'his good pleasure'. Our wonderful God didn't wait for our good pleasure when he saved us, and he is not waiting for our good pleasure to bring us into conformity with his perfect design for us. He is working for *his* good pleasure. Behind this ceaseless, effectual and complete work of our indwelling God, there is all his eternal purpose to save us and have us for himself. He is working for reasons that make sense to him, for a purpose he has mapped out in his own mind.

Paul reminds us, in Philippians 1:6, 'that he who began a good work in you will carry it on to completion until the day of Christ Jesus'. God began the good work in us when he chose us in Christ before the foundation of the world (Ephesians 1:4). Our standing in Christ depends solely on his will. And he will keep working until he finishes the good work on 'the day of Christ'. This means that our complete and final perfection is as certain as God's pledge to his Son to give him the glory. God has said that there is a day coming when Jesus' triumph will be made public and every knee will bow and every tongue confess him as Lord (Philippians 2:10–11). Only the Father knows the timing of that day. But God has promised that, on the day of Christ, he will have us ready; there will be no unsanctified believer. Everything and everybody will be prepared for the glorious triumph that God is preparing for his Son. In the meantime, he will continue putting the finishing touches on his 'good work'.

Sometimes we are discouraged by our slow progress towards holiness. We are keenly aware of our sin and how far short we fall of God's perfect standard. But that's a good sign! The deeper our relationship with God, the more we appreciate his beauty and perfection, and the more sensitive we are to all that offends him. Keep resisting sin, keep striving for holiness. Take heart, God is working in you and will have you ready for the great day of Christ.

> And we all, who with unveiled faces contemplate the Lord's glory, are being transformed into his image with ever-increasing glory, which comes from the Lord, who is the Spirit.
> (2 Corinthians 3:18)

Day 18

Read Philippians 2:1–13
Key verses: Philippians 2:12–13

....

12Therefore, my dear friends, as you have always obeyed – not only in my presence, but now much more in my absence – continue to work out your salvation with fear and trembling, 13for it is God who works in you to will and to act in order to fulfil his good purpose.

If there is a lift to get us to the top of the building, then we don't need to bother to take the stairs. In the same way, if God is working in us to make us perfect on the day of Christ, then surely we should give up the effort and leave it to him?

But Scripture does not say that God is doing it all, therefore we can relax. It says that God is working to this amazing extent in every believer, therefore 'work out your salvation with fear and trembling' – with fear and trembling because we owe a responsibility to the Father who loves us. This is not fear of judgment but fear of displeasing the One who loves us so much.

What does it mean to 'work out your salvation'? We already have full salvation. Christ has made us right with God and, at the cross, our sins were forgiven and we were sanctified. Paul talks about 'your salvation' because it is something we already possess. So, when he says 'work out your salvation', he means that we should appropriate it, to make sure we are growing in our experience of it.

The Old Testament provides a perfect illustration of this. Remember when the Israelites stood on the border of Canaan? This was the land that God had promised to their ancestors. It was already theirs, but now they were charged to 'go in to possess' (Joshua 1:11, KJV). Similarly, after Abraham had separated from Lot, God showed him all the land that he was giving to him and his descendants, and told him to walk the length and breadth of it (Genesis 13:14–17). Abraham was possessing his possession. So, we too have to appropriate, and make real in our personal experience, everything that was accomplished for us on Calvary.

How do we do this? By obedience (Philippians 2:12). We follow the example of Christ (2:6–8). Jesus was in full possession of the divine nature, the outworking of which was a life of self-denial and self-sacrifice. God now lives in us; we are partakers of the divine nature. And just as the possession of the divine nature led Jesus on a self-denying path of submissive obedience to the will of God, so 'as you have always obeyed', carry on the good work.

Obedience is the way we 'work out our salvation' and are confident that we're pleasing God. Don't give up on it or grow weary of it – God is in you, spurring you on to follow in the footsteps of Jesus. Today, with God's help, take the step of obedience that is in front of you – cleaning up your thought life, taking part in a church rota diligently, demonstrating God's love to your children, caring for that elderly relative with respect, and being 'salt and light' to non-Christian friends.

Day 19

Read Colossians 1:1–14
Key verses: Colossians 1:1–2

....

¹*Paul, an apostle of Christ Jesus by the will of God, and Timothy our brother,*

²*To God's holy people in Colossae, the faithful brothers and sisters in Christ:*

Grace and peace to you from God our Father.

Did you know that if you are a believer, you are a saint?

Paul is writing to 'God's holy people [literally 'saints'] in Colossae'. This was a phrase used of the ancient people of God, the Jewish nation. And now, writing both to Jews and Gentiles, Paul says, 'You are saints. You are set apart for God. You belong to him.' You can't make yourself a saint but God can and does for, in the New Testament, it is a term applied to every Christian without exception. And, as saints, we have a dual address: 'To God's holy people *in Colossae*, the faithful brothers and sisters *in Christ'* (emphasis added). Do you see that double emphasis? Christians are people who live at two addresses: they live in Colossae and they live in Christ.

Colossae was in the Lycus Valley, in what is now modern Turkey. It had seen better days. It didn't have the reputation of neighbouring towns such as Hierapolis or Laodicea. It was a bit of a backwater. But God knew the circumstances of these believers in Colossae. I love the verse in Revelation 2:13, written to the Christians in Pergamum: 'I know where you live – where Satan has his throne.' God knows where you live. And where you live will have a certain impact on who you are. Your background, your family, will colour some of your experience of Christ. But here's the key – your background mustn't be the thing that defines you.

Paul says, 'You are the saints in Colossae . . . in Christ.' He uses this phrase 'in Christ' many times in his letters. Why? Because it is the marker for Christian identity. What defines me is not where I've come from but to whom I belong and, as a result, where I am going. My identity is determined not by my gender, sexual orientation, achievements, job or background, but by who I am in Christ. I belong to Jesus – that's my identity.

Being a saint does not, however, negate the struggles of life. That's why Paul says, 'Grace and peace to you from God our Father.' God gives us every grace we need, no matter what the trouble may be. And he provides peace – not merely the absence of war but shalom, God's wholeness and well-being in our hearts and for our lives.

Your 'Colossae', wherever you live, will no doubt have shaped you. But don't let it define you. Your identity is securely based on your union with Christ. You belong to him. As you go through your day, be mindful of who you are and to whom you belong. Receive the grace and peace God has for you today; rely on his resources to live the life God designed you for.

Day 20

Read Colossians 2:20 – 3:17
Key verses: Colossians 3:1–4

....

¹Since, then, you have been raised with Christ, set your hearts on things above, where Christ is, seated at the right hand of God. ²Set your minds on things above, not on earthly things. ³For you died, and your life is now hidden with Christ in God. ⁴When Christ, who is your life, appears, then you also will appear with him in glory.

Imagine a doctor standing by your hospital bed, telling you, 'You're cured. There is no longer any trace of the disease.'

You might not feel cured. In fact, you know that if you got out of bed, you would collapse with weakness. Nevertheless, the reality is that you are cured. In a similar way, as we struggle with sin, we don't always think that we are living the new life of Christ. But the reality is that we are united with Christ, and his finished work on the cross has been accredited to us. We don't need to feel this truth but we do have to believe it.

This passage outlines what is true about every Christian: 'you died with Christ' (2:20); 'you have been raised with Christ' (3:1); 'your life is now hidden with Christ in God' (3:3); 'you also will appear with him in glory' (3:4). What does it mean that when Jesus died, we died? It means that the fully paid penalty for sin has been credited to our account. Jesus' resurrection means that when he rose, the full reality of a new life was credited to us. The Father has granted to us, here and now, the eternal security of a life already established in heaven. We will share the heavenly place; we'll serve him and see his face. But that will not add to our security for, at this present moment, as those who have been identified with Jesus, our lives are hidden with Christ in God. The consummation of all of this will be when we appear with him in glory.

When the Lord appears at his second coming, believers will be shown in their true colours at his side. This is a sure hope. Jesus won't put on any new glory for the occasion. He will show then the glory he possesses *now*. Likewise, we will shine with the glory we have now, which was purchased on Calvary: the glory of the ascended life, the glory that is our true reality at this present moment.

In *Pilgrim's Progress*, John Bunyan describes a man who could look only down:

> One stood above the man's head holding a celestial crown and he offered him that crown for his muck rake; but the man never looked up . . . Instead, he only raked bits of straw, the small sticks, and dust from the floor. (John Bunyan, *Pilgrim's Progress*, Aneko Press, 2015, p. 217)

Stop digging around in the dirt! 'Set your hearts . . . set your minds on things above': you have died and been raised with Christ; your life is hidden with Christ in God, and you will appear with him in glory. A heavenly crown and glory are yours.

Reflect on these truths; be confident in them and live as if you believe them.

Day 21

Read 1 Thessalonians 2:1–20
Key verse: 1 Thessalonians 2:18

•••

We wanted to come to you – certainly I, Paul, did, again and again – but Satan blocked our way.

Are you confident of God's authority over Satan? Alternatively, do you look at your life and what is going on in the world and wonder if Satan is running amok?

Clearly, there is a supernatural power ranged against believers, but we need to have a sense of proportion. In Paul's letters, Satan is mentioned by name only nine times. Compare that with the hundreds of times that Paul refers to 'Jesus', 'the Lord Jesus' and 'Jesus Christ'. We also need to remember that Satan does not operate as a free agent, but only within the sovereign purposes of God. Even in Revelation 20, where Satan is let loose, it is only to do what God predetermined he should do.

The opening chapters of Job explain this to us. It wasn't Satan who said, 'I'm going to have a go at your servant Job.' No, it was the Lord who said, 'Have you considered my servant Job?' (Job 1:8). And it was God who put the boundary markers in place. Satan could touch Job's children, home, goods and even his health, but not his life. Somehow, great eternal issues are at stake here. The point is that Satan could only operate within the permission, direction and limitation of God.

Here in 1 Thessalonians 2, Paul wanted to go back to see the believers, but he says that Satan put a roadblock in his way. God allowed Satan to prevent Paul's visit. We don't know how he did it. But wasn't it good that Paul could not return to Thessalonica? As a result, he learned first-hand that our spiritual welfare rests in the hands of God, who is looking after his church.

It is well to remember that Satan's power is not inherent, but permitted (Rom. 13:1). It is not unlimited, but controlled (Job 1:12; 2:6). It is not invincible, but broken (Luke 11:21–22). It is not assured of success, but is surely doomed (Rev. 20:2–3). Satan knows well that there is no ultimate victory for him. The pronounced sentence has only been postponed. But he works to hinder and postpone Christ's final triumph. We can rejoice in the

certainty of John's assurance: 'Greater is he that is in you, than he that is in the world' (1 John 4:4).
(J. Oswald Sanders, *Cultivation of Christian Character*, Moody Press, 1965, p. 86)

Heavenly Father, when it seems as if Satan has the upper hand, help me to remember that you are on the throne and in control, and that he operates only within the boundaries you have permitted. When I can't see how you are working, or why you have allowed Satan to turn his attention on me, help me to trust you. And if there are lessons you want me to learn, help me to learn them well and not to miss the opportunity to sink deeper roots into Christ. Amen.

1 John

John, the apostle and author of the Gospel of John and Revelation, wrote this letter to be circulated among the churches in the province of Asia, into which an early form of Gnosticism was infiltrating. This heresy taught that spirit is entirely good and matter is entirely evil. As it didn't matter what you did with your body, breaking God's law was of no consequence, so a lack of morality ruled. Salvation was seen as an escape from the body, not by faith in Jesus Christ but by possessing special knowledge. John wrote to oppose this false teaching and assure believers that they were truly saved: 'I write these things to you who believe in the name of the Son of God so that you may know that you have eternal life' (5:13). His first letter points us to Jesus' death on the cross as the grounds for our unshakeable confidence in God's love and our salvation.

Day 22

Read 1 John 4:7–21
Key verse: 1 John 4:17

•••

This is how love is made complete among us so that we will have confidence on the day of judgment: in this world we are like Jesus.

Are you ever tongue-tied in certain stressful situations?

Maybe you just can't find the right words to say when a particular relative or work colleague comes into the room. If any situation is going to leave us tongue-tied and cause us to hang our heads in shame, surely it will be the day of judgment (Revelation 6:15–17). But John says that God's love is designed to give us confidence on that day. God's love is 'made complete' – in other words, it has accomplished its goal, reached its target in us, when we have confidence to face the day of judgment. The word 'confidence' conveys the idea of outspokenness, of freedom of speech.

How can we have this type of confidence? Verse 17 of 1 John 4 says that 'in this world we are like Jesus'. John writes as if we are just like Jesus, as if our relationship with the Father is just like his. Jesus doesn't come cringing and fearful into his Father's presence, and neither should we: 1 John 3:1–2 reminds us that we are not just *called* 'children of God' but that we *are* 'children of God'. Similarly, Romans 8:16–17 tell us that we are children of God and so 'heirs of God and co-heirs with Christ'. What he inherits, so shall we inherit. Because we are God's children, we can stand in his presence on the last day.

Clearly, there are differences between us and Christ. One of the tensions between John and his opponents concerned the sense in which we are like Jesus. The opponents wanted to view themselves as little Christs. But John emphasizes that, unlike Jesus, we are not in glory yet. Judgment day is not behind us but ahead of us. In this world, we are not beyond the reach of sin, but we are cleansed from all unrighteousness. This is where we stake our confidence for the day of judgment: 'If we confess our sins, he is faithful and just and will forgive us our sins and purify us from all unrighteousness' (1 John 1:9). Indeed, God's love has accomplished its goal in us when we are confident on the day of judgment because we know we're cleansed from all unrighteousness.

Nobody can produce new evidence of your depravity that will make God change his mind. For God justified you with (so to speak) his eyes open. He knew the worst about you at the time when he accepted you for Jesus' sake; and the verdict which he passed then was, and is, final.
(J. I. Packer, *Knowing God*, Hodder & Stoughton, 2005, p. 310)

Are you worried about judgment day? There is no need to be. We can be confident, not because of our own goodness and achievements but because Christ's sacrifice declares us righteous (Romans 3:22–24). It also guarantees that God will give us the same welcome he gave Christ. And as we grow in love and become more like Jesus, this is further assurance that we're saved – yet more reason to be confident as we approach that final day.

In the meantime, keep coming to God for forgiveness, press on in love and obedience, becoming what you are – righteous in his sight.

Day 23

Read 1 John 4:7–21
Key verse: 1 John 4:18

••

There is no fear in love. But perfect love drives out fear, because fear has to do with punishment. The one who fears is not made perfect in love.

What is your biggest fear?

There is a right fear of God that we all ought to have. That is, treating him as God, as maker and sustainer of all, our Saviour and Sovereign to whom every one of us needs to give an account. But the fear John mentions here is linked to terror and punishment; it is a fear of what God might do to us. This type of fear has no place in Christian life because God's love drives it away.

When John describes God's love in this chapter, it's always in terms of the cross. God's love is no romantic gesture: it is practical and purposeful. So, 1 John 4:9–10 says:

This is how God showed his love among us: he sent his one and only Son into the world that we might live through him. This is love: not that we loved God, but that he loved us and sent his Son as an atoning sacrifice for our sins.

God demonstrates his love by sending Jesus to die for my sin and giving me eternal life. And, if I have eternal life, I don't need to fear eternal death. If my sins have been atoned for, I don't need to be terrified, even of a holy God. If I'm saved, I needn't be frightened about the day of judgment.

John is not asking us to believe that we're lovely enough for God. He's not even telling us that, if we love God enough, we can have confidence on that day. When John speaks of love, he's not thinking of our feelings at all but pointing us back to the cross. And when we look at the cross, we have assurance of eternal life.

Some of us are so conscious of our sins and shame that we almost refuse to believe that this confidence can be ours. But don't be more concerned about your sin than you are about God's love. Jesus says, 'Remain in my love' (John 15:9). Believe it and apply it to your heart each day, because this love was designed to give you confidence on the day of judgment.

For God so loved the world that he gave his one and only Son, that whoever believes in him shall not perish but have eternal life.

(John 3:16)

Unless we're very intentional about meditating on these truths [that show God's love], they slip from our thoughts like misty dreams that evaporate in the morning light. That's why Luther said we must 'take heed then, to embrace . . . the love and kindness of God . . . [and] daily exercise [our] faith therein'.

(Elyse M. Fitzpatrick, *Because He Loves Me*, Crossway, 2010, p. 36)

Today, look to the cross and revel in God's love for you. Believe it, and stake your past, present and future on it. Let it banish your fear.

Revelation

As early as the end of the first century, the future of the church hung in the balance. False teaching and internal division were rife. Domitian, the Roman emperor, had instigated persecution against those who would not worship him as lord. The apostle John, exiled on the island of Patmos, wrote to encourage believers to resist the demands of the emperor. He exhorted them to stand firm against the devil's schemes, secure in the knowledge that God was with them and that, one day soon, they would be vindicated.

Written in an apocalyptic style, the book of Revelation is full of highly symbolic visions that can seem strange to us. We won't understand every detail, but the certainty of Christ's triumphant return comes across loudly and clearly, so we can be confident in God's sovereignty and love, as well as our salvation and glorious future.

Day 24

Read Revelation 1:4–8
Key verses: Revelation 1:5–6

....

[5]To him who loves us and has freed us from our sins by his blood, [6]and has made us to be a kingdom and priests to serve his God and Father – to him be glory and power for ever and ever! Amen.

Jesus loves you! Have you got that message by now?

John writes, 'To him who loves us . . .' What a message for these first-century believers. Many who received this letter were slaves; they had no assurance of love; they could not look back to parents or family who loved them. They were flawed; they encountered difficulties. You only need to read Revelation 2 – 3 to realize that these were not model believers. And yet, despite all that, they, like us, could be confident of Jesus' love in all its glorious dimensions.

- *It is a costly love.* There is sacrifice at the heart of this love. It is not the love of a teacher who has marvellous ideas, although Jesus is the most superb teacher the world has ever known. It is not the love of someone who displays a glorious, morally upright example, although Jesus certainly did that. It is the love of someone who paid the greatest price ever, who demonstrated his love by giving himself to die in our place. The cross of Christ shows us not only the depravity of people but also the dignity of humankind. We are made in the image of God and, in the heart and mind of God, we are worth saving.

- *It is an unrequited love.* 'You have persevered and have endured hardships for my name . . . Yet I hold this against you: you have forsaken the love you had at first' (Revelation 2:3–4). Believers in Ephesus, like many of us, had understood the costly love of Christ and yet abandoned it. For all their many gifts, talents and skills, they had lost the thing that matters most of all.

- *It is a corrective love.* 'Those whom I love I rebuke and discipline' (Revelation 3:19). Jesus loves us enough to rebuke and chastise us. When you fail him, he still loves you and goes on loving you. He doesn't love you for the love he gets back, but because he can't help loving you; it is in his nature to love you. And he loves you so much that he corrects you.

Notice this love is in the present tense. It is not that he loved us once, at the cross, and demonstrated it by the shedding of his blood. No, he loves us today with the same love that drove him to Calvary. Although our love falters, his remains the same.

You can be confident of this: Jesus loves you. Nothing – no circumstances, no sin – can separate you from his love (Romans 8:38).

The gospel is this: We are more sinful and flawed in ourselves than we ever dared believe, yet at the very same time we are more loved and accepted in Jesus Christ than we ever dared hope.
(Timothy Keller with Kathy Keller, *The Meaning of Marriage*, Hodder & Stoughton, 2011, p. 48)

Day 25

Read Revelation 1:4–8
Key verses: Revelation 1:5–6

•••

5To him who loves us and has freed us from our sins by his blood, 6and has made us to be a kingdom and priests to serve his God and Father – to him be glory and power for ever and ever! Amen.

Freedom!

We all want it, but not many of us experience it. In the first century, a number of people were captive as slaves; others were bound by traditions. Today, people still need liberating from a host of different tyrannies. And Christ is the only liberator. Even as believers, we frequently have to be reminded of the freedom we have in Christ.

In these opening chapters of Revelation, we see that the freedom Christ brings has both a negative and a positive element. Here in Revelation 1:5, it is freedom *from* our sins. The positive element comes in verse 6, which explains what we have been freed *for*: '[Christ] has made us to be a kingdom and priests to serve his God and Father – to him be glory and power for ever and ever! Amen.'

Revelation 5:9–10 portrays a similar scene. In his vision, John sees the living creatures and elders singing a new song to Christ:

> You are worthy to take the scroll
> > and to open its seals,
> because you were slain,
> > and with your blood you purchased for God
> > persons from every tribe and language and
> > > people and nation.
> You have made them to be a kingdom and priests
> > to serve our God,
> > and they will reign on the earth.

We can be confident that Christ's work on the cross and mighty resurrection free us from the bondage to sin and guilt, from the things that held us captive in the past, from the habitual sins we struggle with, and from the sins we have committed today and will do tomorrow (Ephesians 1:7). But we can also be confident that we are redeemed for a purpose – 'for God'. He has made us 'a kingdom and priests'. There is an echo here of Exodus 19:6, when God brought the Israelites out of slavery in

Egypt: 'you will be for me a kingdom of priests and a holy nation'. We are now members of a privileged kingdom. Our response must be to acknowledge the King's rule over every part of our lives – work, home, church and leisure. It doesn't stop there, for God has also made us priests to worship and serve him for the rest of our days. This is true freedom.

Today, live confidently in the freedom Christ has won for you – no longer shackled by the guilt of past sin, but choosing to obey God at every opportunity you get.

Since we're free in the freedom of God, can we do anything that comes to mind? Hardly. You know well enough from your own experience that there are some acts of so-called freedom that destroy freedom. Offer yourselves to sin, for instance, and it's your last free act. But offer yourselves to the ways of God and the freedom never quits. All your lives you've let sin tell you what to do. But thank God you've started listening to a new master, one whose commands set you free to live openly in *his* freedom!

(Romans 6:17–18, MSG)

Day 26

Read Revelation 2:8–11
Key verse: Revelation 2:8

••

To the angel of the church in Smyrna write:

These are the words of him who is the First and the Last, who died and came to life again.

Have you received a personal letter recently? A hand-written envelope with a postage stamp?

It is much more significant than a generic email, isn't it? Perhaps unsurprisingly, Jesus' letters to the seven churches in Revelation 2 – 3 are personalized. In each, the designation or reference given to Christ is specifically appropriate to the situation of that church. Many of the phrases introducing Christ are borrowed from the earlier vision in Revelation 1.

When writing to Smyrna, the designation is: 'These are the words of him who is the First and the Last, who died and came to life again.' The phrase 'the First and the Last' is used of God himself in Isaiah 44:6. John uses it in Revelation 1:17, and also at the end of the book. Jesus, God's Son, is at the beginning and at the end. He is the Lord of life. Here (in Revelation 2:8), the tense of the verb refers to the moment of resurrection: 'he became dead and lived again'. The Christians in Smyrna would have listened attentively. They were living in a city that had been destroyed and rebuilt, that had died and been resurrected. And now death hung over them. So, the words of the One who had defeated death represented another great assurance, another great certainty in their Christian discipleship.

Similarly, our hope for the future is based on an event that has already happened. Usually, our hopes are to do with something that has not yet occurred. We look at possibilities and say, 'I hope it will be sunny tomorrow.' But there are no guarantees. Christian hope is radically different. It *will* be realized. It is totally certain. Why? Because it is based on an event that has already happened. We have hope because of the resurrection of Jesus Christ from the dead (1 Peter 1:3). Jesus died and sprang to life again; he is the First and the Last; he is the Lord of life – so we can be confident of death's defeat and of our resurrection.

'Everything will be all right in the end. If it's not all right, it's not the end' (Sonny, in the film *The Best Exotic Marigold Hotel*). Things were not all right for those suffering believers in Smyrna. But they, like us, can look forward with certainty to a day when everything will be all right – more than all right, absolutely perfect! Remember, we can be confident of our glorious future because Jesus defeated death, and his resurrection blazed the trail for us.

I am the resurrection and the life. The one who believes in me will live, even though they die.
(John 11:25)

I am the Living One; I was dead, and now look, I am alive for ever and ever! And I hold the keys of death and Hades.
(Revelation 1:18)

Day 27

Read Revelation 2:8–11
Key verse: Revelation 2:9

•••

I know your afflictions and your poverty – yet you are
rich! I know about the slander of those who say they
are Jews and are not, but are a synagogue of Satan.

'I know . . .'

Jesus knew all about these believers. He knew that they
were destitute. He knew that they were being slandered
by members of the Jewish synagogue following their
conversion. He knew the persecution, imprisonment and
even death that members of this small Christian com-
munity would face.

How did Jesus know? In John's vision (Revelation 1), we
are told that Jesus walks among the lampstands – among
the churches. He is with his people.

Down through the ages, God's people have testified to
this truth. Paul, in a Roman dungeon, cold, lonely, deserted

and close to martyrdom, stated, 'The Lord stood by my side and gave me strength' (2 Timothy 4:17). The Puritan Richard Baxter (1615–1691) wrote a hymn ('Lord, it belongs not to my care') that contains the line 'Christ leads me through no darker rooms than he went through before'. Betsie ten Boom, incarcerated in Ravensbrück concentration camp, said to her sister Corrie, 'We must tell people . . . that there is no pit so deep that he is not deeper still' (Corrie ten Boom with John and Elizabeth Sherill, *The Hiding Place*, Hodder & Stoughton, 2004, p. 202).

Today, we face demanding pressures and carry debilitating burdens. The costs of discipleship are very real. So please don't miss the comforting certainty of Christ's presence. What gives such pressure its meaning is our vital connection with Jesus. We suffer in solidarity with Jesus, who took our sufferings upon himself.

The late Helen Roseveare was a medical missionary in the Democratic Republic of Congo. During the uprisings of the 1960s, she endured beatings, torture and rape. She told of one occasion when, as she was close to being executed, the Holy Spirit reminded her of her calling:

Twenty years ago, you asked me for the privilege of being identified with me. This is it. Don't you want it? This is what it means. These are not your sufferings. All I ask of you is the loan of your body.

She was spared execution and later wrote:

He didn't stop the sufferings. He didn't stop the wickedness, the cruelties, the humiliation or anything. It was all there. The pain was just as bad. The fear was just as bad. But it was altogether different. It was in Jesus, for him, with him.

(Quoted in Philip Ryken, *The Message of Salvation*, IVP, 2001, p. 257)

The great certainty for those Christians in Smyrna, and for us, is that no matter what happens, the suffering and risen Christ is with us.

You are not alone. Through every trial, doubt and discouragement, God is with you. There is no situation too awful, no doubt too shocking, no failure too final to separate you from God. Lean on the truth of God's word:

The LORD himself goes before you and will be with you; he will never leave you nor forsake you. Do not be afraid; do not be discouraged.
(Deuteronomy 31:8)

Day 28

Read Revelation 2:8–11
Key verse: Revelation 2:10

● ●

Do not be afraid of what you are about to suffer. I tell you, the devil will put some of you in prison to test you, and you will suffer persecution for ten days. Be faithful, even to the point of death, and I will give you life as your victor's crown.

Do you ever wonder why God allows you to suffer? Why you seem to be under such sustained attack?

Some believers live as if they are in a *Star Wars* adventure. They assume that they are surrounded by equal and opposite forces of good and evil. Neither good nor evil is quite strong enough, so they assign this part of life, or this event, exclusively to God and another part to the devil. It is almost as if there were two worlds of good and evil, with their lives swinging between the two. Other Christians believe that God is good, and whenever something evil enters their lives, God must remove it in response to the prayer of faith. If the evil doesn't disappear, it is because their faith is weak. Neither of these is a biblical perspective but, surprisingly, each is a common feature of supposed Christian spirituality.

It is clear from the New Testament that Christians experience satanic resistance. Twice in this short letter to the church in Smyrna, the risen Christ refers to Satan's work. In verse 9, Satan has inspired the actions of some Jews and, in verse 10, it is he who will put some of the Christians in prison. In verse 10, he is referred to as 'the devil', which means the accuser or slanderer, the 'father of lies' (John 8:44).

We can easily forget that there is a devil actively working against us, and that Christian discipleship is lived out in the context of a spiritual battle. But these verses make clear that this evil is not out of control. Notice that only some of the believers were put in prison, and the persecution was for a defined period. There were limits imposed. As in the story of Job, the situation was still under the Lord's oversight and care. We can be confident that nothing lies outside the scope of God's sovereignty and control, not even Satan. He can act only within the parameters that God has set.

No trouble, no hardship and no suffering can touch you, unless God, in his infinite wisdom, has allowed it. Imagine God sifting troubles through his hand like grains of sand. Some troubles he will keep from you, others he will allow into your life, with the express purpose of moulding you into the image of his Son. Today, be confident in God's good purposes for you.

I make known the end from the beginning,
    from ancient times, what is still to come.
I say, 'My purpose will stand,
    and I will do all that I please.'
(Isaiah 46:10)

Who can speak and have it happen
    if the Lord has not decreed it?
Is it not from the mouth of the Most High
    that both calamities and good things come?
(Lamentations 3:37–38)

Day 29

Read Revelation 2:8–11
Key verses: Revelation 2:10–11

•••

¹⁰Do not be afraid of what you are about to suffer. I tell you, the devil will put some of you in prison to test you, and you will suffer persecution for ten days. Be faithful, even to the point of death, and I will give you life as your victor's crown.

¹¹Whoever has ears, let them hear what the Spirit says to the churches. The one who is victorious will not be hurt at all by the second death.

Eighty and six years have I served him and he has done me no wrong. How then can I blaspheme my king who saved me?
(*Polycarp's Letter to the Philippians and His Martyrdom*, CreateSpace, 2016, p. 19)

These were the words of Polycarp, the leader of the small church in Smyrna, when he was commanded to hail Caesar as lord. Many years after John's letter had arrived, Polycarp was martyred, as Jesus had predicted in verse 10. Like countless others, he forfeited his reward in this life because of his confidence in something far better.

For him and for us, the promised reward is a 'crown of life' (verse 10, ESV). This is possibly the image of the crown of victory in the games or a laurel crown as a reward for service in the city. But it probably refers to the royal crown, the reward to faithful disciples who will rule with Christ.

And not only that, verse 11 assures us that the faithful disciple 'will not be hurt at all by the second death'. This phrase is used by John later in Revelation, which helps us to understand its meaning: 'Then death and Hades were thrown into the lake of fire. The lake of fire is the second death' (Revelation 20:14). The second death is by eternal judgment. It is the death after death. We will all die once, but the second death is an eternity separated from God. And for Christ's followers, this death will not touch us. It is an emphatic double negative in verse 11. There is no way you will ultimately be harmed. You are absolutely secure.

It is costly to be a disciple of Christ. As Paul and Barnabas reminded new believers, 'We must go through many hardships to enter the kingdom of God' (Acts 14:22). But troubles are not a dead end; rather, they are the gateway to life in all its fullness. So, 'Do not be afraid . . . Be faithful' (Revelation 2:10) because 'if we endure, we will also reign with him' (2 Timothy 2:12).

God is not oblivious to what it is costing you to follow him. He sees all your sacrifices, the acts of obedience no one else sees. Today, have confidence in his promise: one day you will be rewarded for your deeds of faith. You will receive a crown of life to lay at the feet of your Saviour whom you have loved and served.

Blessed is the one who perseveres under trial because, having stood the test, that person will receive the crown of life that the Lord has promised to those who love him.

(James 1:12)

Day 30

Read Revelation 4:1–11
Key verses: Revelation 4:1–2

....

¹After this I looked, and there before me was a door standing open in heaven. And the voice I had first heard speaking to me like a trumpet said, 'Come up here, and I will show you what must take place after this.' ²At once I was in the Spirit, and there before me was a throne in heaven with someone sitting on it.

We know we need a physical health check once in a while, but have you had a spiritual check-up lately?

In Revelation 2 and 3, the Lord has been giving the church a spiritual check-up. There are lots of wonderful things to commend, but there are also some serious problems and challenges to address. The church is under attack; virtually all the seven churches are facing persecution. They are being invaded by false teachers, people who bring what the writer calls the deep teaching of Satan

(Revelation 2:24). The spiritual decline within the churches is almost bordering on apostasy.

To the church in Sardis, God says, 'You have such a fantastic reputation! Everyone's talking about how alive you are. But it is only a reputation. You're spiritually dead.' To the church in Laodicea, he says, 'You are so compromised, you make me sick.' You can imagine the apostle John looking at the state of the church, hearing this word from the Lord and wondering, 'Has the church got a future?' And it is after these things that God takes John to heaven and shows him the great and glorious vision recorded in chapter four.

What is the point of this vision? To remind us that when the church is feeble and the world seems to have turned its back on God completely, the ultimate place of authority in the universe is the throne of God. And it is occupied. It has never been unoccupied. The word 'throne' is one of the key words in Revelation. It is used about sixty times in the New Testament, forty-seven of them in the book of Revelation and fourteen times in this chapter. The theme of this chapter and, indeed, the whole Bible is the absolute authority of the throne of God. We can be confident of this: when the church is in a state and things are going badly, God is still on the throne.

Father, our lives are broken. We're serving in difficult situations, and sometimes it feels as if the world is spinning out of control. It is so easy to become anxious, despondent and filled with doubt. Thank you that things are not as they appear. You are on the throne, high and exalted. You love us and are in control. Today, grant us peace in knowing you reign, faith that keeps our hearts focused on Christ, and hope because one day your authority will be gloriously on display and everyone will bow before you. Until that day, may our words and actions testify to Christ's rule in our lives and point others to the gospel. Amen.

For further study

If you would like to read more on the theme of confidence in Christ, you might find this selection of books helpful.

On the theme of assurance of salvation and our eternal destiny:

- Joel R. Beeke, *Knowing and Growing in Assurance of Faith* (Christian Focus, 2017).

- Ray Galea, *From Here to Eternity: Assurance in the face of sin and suffering* (Matthias Media, 2017).

- Greg Gilbert, *Assured: Discover grace, let go of guilt, and rest in your salvation* (Baker, 2019).

On the theme of confidence in God's love despite our failures:

- Matt Fuller, *Perfect Sinners: See yourself as God sees you* (The Good Book Company, 2017).

On the theme of confidence in God's sovereignty:

- Christopher Ash, *Where Was God When That Happened? And other questions about God's goodness, power and the way he works in the world* (The Good Book Company, 2017).

- Orlando Saer, *Big God: How to approach suffering, spread the gospel, make decisions and pray in the light of a God who really is in the driving seat of the world* (Christian Focus, 2014).

On the theme of dealing with doubt:

- John Stevens, *How Can I Be Sure? And other questions about doubt, assurance and the Bible* (The Good Book Company, 2014).

On the theme of confidence in the Scriptures:

- Daniel Strange and Michael Ovey, *Confident: Why we can trust the Bible* (Christian Focus, 2015).

- Lee Strobel, *The Case for Christ: A journalist's personal investigation of the evidence for Jesus* (Zondervan, 2016).

- Peter J. Williams, *Can We Trust the Gospels?* (Crossway, 2018).

Keswick Ministries

Our purpose

Keswick Ministries exists to inspire and equip Christians to love and live for Christ in his world.

God's purpose is to bring his blessing to all the nations of the world (Genesis 12:3). That promise of blessing, which touches every aspect of human life, is ultimately fulfilled through the life, death, resurrection, ascension and future return of Christ. All the people of God are called to participate in his missionary purposes, wherever he may place them. The central vision of Keswick Ministries is to see the people of God equipped, inspired and refreshed to fulfil that calling, directed and guided by God's Word in the power of his Spirit, for the glory of his Son.

Our priorities

There are three fundamental priorities which shape all that we do as we look to serve the local church.

- *Hearing God's Word*: the Scriptures are the foundation for the church's life, growth and mission, and Keswick Ministries is committed to preach and teach God's

Word in a way that is faithful to Scripture and relevant to Christians of all ages and backgrounds.

- *Becoming like God's Son*: from its earliest days, the Keswick movement has encouraged Christians to live godly lives in the power of the Spirit, to grow in Christ-likeness and to live under his Lordship in every area of life. This is God's will for his people in every culture and generation.

- *Serving God's mission*: the authentic response to God's Word is obedience to his mission, and the inevitable result of Christlikeness is sacrificial service. Keswick Ministries seeks to encourage committed discipleship in family life, work and society, and energetic engagement in the cause of world mission.

Our ministry

- *Keswick Convention*. The Convention attracts some 12,000 to 15,000 Christians from the UK and around the world to Keswick every summer. It provides Bible teaching for all ages, vibrant worship, a sense of unity across generations and denominations, and an inspirational call to serve Christ in the world. It caters for children of all ages and has a strong youth and young adult programme. And it all takes place in the beautiful

Lake District – a perfect setting for rest, recreation and refreshment.

- *Keswick fellowship.* For more than 140 years, the work of Keswick has affected churches worldwide, not just through individuals being changed but also through Bible conventions that originate or draw their inspiration from the Keswick Convention. Today, there is a network of events that share Keswick Ministries' priorities across the UK and in many parts of Europe, Asia, North America, Australia, Africa and the Caribbean. Keswick Ministries is committed to strengthening the network in the UK and beyond through prayer, news and co-operative activity.

- *Keswick teaching and training.* Keswick Ministries is developing a range of inspiring, Bible-centred teaching and training that focuses on equipping believers for 'whole-of-life' discipleship. This builds on the same concern that started the Convention, that all Christians live godly lives in the power of the Spirit in all spheres of life in God's world. Some of the smaller and more intensive events focus on equipping attendees, while others focus on inspiring them. Some are for pastors, others for those in different forms of church leadership, while many are for any Christian. The aim of all the courses is for the participants to return home refreshed to serve.

- *Keswick resources*. Keswick Ministries produces a range of books, devotionals, study guides and digital resources to inspire and equip the church to live for Christ. The printed resources focus on the core foundations of Christian life and mission, and help the people of God in their walk with Christ. The digital resources make teaching and sung worship from the Keswick Convention available in a variety of ways.

Our unity
The Keswick movement worldwide has adopted a key Pauline statement to describe its gospel inclusivity: 'All one in Christ Jesus' (Galatians 3:28). Keswick Ministries works with evangelicals from a wide variety of church backgrounds, on the understanding that they share a commitment to the essential truths of the Christian faith as set out in our statement of belief.

Our contact details
T: 017687 80075
E: info@keswickministries.org
W: www.keswickministries.org
Mail: Keswick Ministries, Rawnsley Centre, Main Street, Keswick, Cumbria CA12 5NP, England

Related titles from IVP

Food for the Journey

The Food for the Journey series offers daily devotionals from much loved Bible teachers at the Keswick Convention in an ideal pocket-sized format – to accompany you wherever you go.

Available in the series

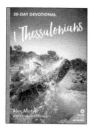  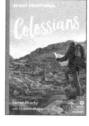 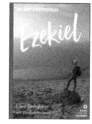

1 Thessalonians

Alec Motyer with
Elizabeth McQuoid
978 1 78359 439 9

2 Timothy

Michael Baughen with
Elizabeth McQuoid
978 1 78359 438 2

Colossians

Steve Brady with
Elizabeth McQuoid
978 1 78359 722 2

Ezekiel

Liam Goligher with
Elizabeth McQuoid
978 1 78359 603 4

 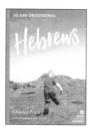  

Habakkuk

Jonathan Lamb with
Elizabeth McQuoid
978 1 78359 652 2

Hebrews

Charles Price with
Elizabeth McQuoid
978 1 78359 611 9

James

Stuart Briscoe with
Elizabeth McQuoid
978 1 78359 523 5

John 14 - 17

Simon Manchester with
Elizabeth McQuoid
978 1 78359 495 5

Available from your local Christian bookshop or **www.ivpbooks.com**

Food for the Journey

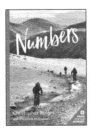   

Numbers

Christopher Wright with Elizabeth McQuoid

978 1 78359 720 8

Revelation 1 - 3

Paul Mallard with Elizabeth McQuoid

978 1 78359 712 3

Romans 5 - 8

John Stott with Elizabeth McQuoid

978 1 78359 718 5

Ruth

Alistair Begg with Elizabeth McQuoid

978 1 78359 525 9

Praise for the series

'This devotional series is biblically rich, theologically deep and full of wisdom . . . I recommend it highly.' **Becky Manley Pippert, speaker, author of** *Out of the Saltshaker and into the World* **and creator of the Live/Grow/Know course and series of books**

'These devotional guides are excellent tools.' **John Risbridger, Minister and Team Leader, Above Bar Church, Southampton**

'These bite-sized banquets . . . reveal our loving Father weaving the loose and messy ends of our everyday lives into his beautiful, eternal purposes in Christ.' **Derek Burnside, Principal, Capernwray Bible School**

'I would highly recommend this series of 30-day devotional books to anyone seeking a tool that will help [him or her] to gain a greater love of Scripture, or just simply . . . to do something out of devotion. Whatever your motivation, these little books are a must-read.' **Claud Jackson,** *Youthwork* **Magazine**

Food for the Journey THEMES

The **Food for the Journey: Themes** series offers offers daily devotions from much loved Bible teachers at the Keswick Convention, exploring how particular themes are woven through the Bible and what we can learn from them today. In a convenient, pocket-sized format, these little books are ideal to accompany you wherever you go.

Available in the series

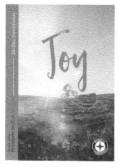

Joy
978 1 78974 163 6
'A rich feast!'
Edrie Mallard

Persevere
978 1 78974 102 5
'Full of essential theology.'
Catherine Campbell

Pray
978 1 78974 169 8
'The ideal reboot.'
Julian Hardyman

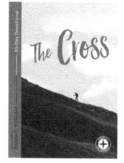

The Cross
978 1 78974 191 9
'A must-read.'
Gavin Calver

Confident
978 1 78974 190 2
'A beautiful collection.'
Elinor Magowan

Related teaching CD and DVD packs

DVD PACKS

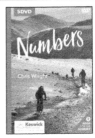  

Colossians
SWP2318A (4-DVD pack)

Ezekiel
SWP2263A (5-DVD pack)

Habakkuk
SWP2299A (5-DVD pack)

John 14 - 17
SWP2238A (5-DVD pack)

Numbers
SWP2317A (5-DVD pack)

Revelation
SWP2300A (5-DVD pack)

Ruth
SWP2280A (5-DVD pack)